CAPE HUNTING DOGS   CHEETAH

THE BOOK OF
ANIMALS
Hamlyn
London   New York   Sydney   Toronto

VERVET MONKEY   KUDU   WILDEBEESTE

CONTENTS

KV-027-444

COVER ARTWORK BY NEMO

© FLEETWAY PUBLICATIONS LTD. 1966.

Printed in Italy by OFSA - Casarile (Milano)

THE AFRICAN LION AND ELEPHANTS

An elephant has a thick, tough skin, but does not like hot sunshine. It uses its trunk to spray water or dust on its back to keep itself cool.

The hot parts of the World nearest to the Equator are called the tropics and most of the great continent of Africa lies within these areas. In fact, Africa has the largest amount of tropical land in the World, so it is not surprising that it also has the largest collection of wild animals, of all kinds and sizes. The African elephant is the biggest land-living animal in the World. Africa's open plains are the home of the antelope, giraffe, zebra, wild ass, rhinoceros, lion, leopard and hyena, to list just a few. The picture opposite shows a scene on one of the great plains of East Africa, beneath the snow-capped Kilimanjaro mountain, which was once an active volcano. Vultures, Thompson's gazelles, Sable antelopes, Rhinoceros, Wildbeeste, Zebras and Warthog are in the background. In front, the lordly Lion and his family rest in the shade of the trees. The male lion looks a very grand sight, with its powerful body and the thick mane of hair which grows on its head and shoulders. Its deep roar, echoing like thunder across the plains at night can be a terrifying sound to other animals— but it is the lioness which does most of the hunting and killing, while the lion roams the plains, growling and roaring to drive frightened deer and other animals in her direction. A lion walks on its toes and in spite of its size, it makes no sound. Its claws are drawn up inside the pads of its feet, so that they do not get worn down, or make a tell-tale clicking sound, as it walks. A group of lions is known as a pride of lions.

African elephants, the biggest animals which live on land, may grow to over eleven feet tall. They have large ears, as much as nine feet across from tip to tip. Although they are huge and weigh about six tons, they can move so softly that they cannot be heard, because their feet are like big, flat, padded cushions. A baby elephant is called a calf. Its mother looks after it very carefully and will defend it bravely against all enemies, but when it is naughty, she will prod it with her tusks (as she is doing in the picture below) or even use her long trunk to spank it. Elephants cannot see very well and in spite of their big ears their hearing is not good, so they have to rely on their keen sense of smell to warn them of danger.

Continued on page 6

Elephants also roll in mud, which dries on their hides and protects them from hot sun, flies and insects.

Because this calf is slow and unwilling to move, the mother elephant prods it with her tusks and nudges it along by butting it with her head.

An Indian elephant wearing its colourful State robes. On its back rides the mahout, or driver. Once trained, elephants become very obedient.

This African elephant fancies some of the top leaves of a tree and easily pushes it over.

Continued from previous page.

The elephant is unusual, because its nose has become a long, movable trunk. This trunk has a keen sense of smell and an acute sense of touch. It is one of the most sensitive parts of an elephant, which hates having its trunk touched. Elephants are vegetarians, which means that they eat only things like leaves, twigs and grass. These are picked up by the animal's trunk and put into its mouth. When an elephant wants to drink, it draws water up into its trunk and then squirts the water down its throat. The African elephant in the picture above is uprooting a tree by pushing against it with its head and front feet. Notice how its trunk is carefully curled back, out of the way. Another place where elephants are found is the sub-continent of India. The Indian kind of elephant is smaller than the African, but the main point of difference is the size of the ears, much smaller in Indian elephants. Indian elephants are greatly used by men for dragging heavy loads or carrying goods. They are still used at times in State processions and are decorated with rich trappings. Their sharp, ivory tusks are shortened and the blunt ends are capped with gold. To capture wild elephants and train them for work is a long and difficult business, for they are very shy and great care has to be taken not to alarm them. The herds of wild elephants live among the tall forests, where the bamboo plants grow thickly and provide them with food. Hunters, trying to capture some of them, may trail them for days. Tame elephants are used to help the hunters and when captured, a wild elephant seems to be content to be led away by them.

Three tame Indian elephants, ridden by hunters, lead back a captured wild elephant. When tamed and trained, wild elephants seem to understand at once the different things the drivers say.

THE GRACEFUL ANTELOPES

The Impalas, which live in South Africa, move around in large herds. They are swift runners, covering the ground in long, graceful leaps, which helps them to escape from their enemies, the big flesh-eating wild cats, such as lions.

The Gerenuik is found in the drier parts of East Africa. It is easy to see why it is called by another name—the Giraffe Antelope—by reason of its long legs and neck. The Gerenuik uses these to reach up and feed on fruits, berries, leaves and young tree shoots.

Africa is really the home of graceful antelopes, although a few are found in places like India. Another name for antelopes might be swift runners. All their life they live in danger from attack by the big cats, such as the lion. They have become good examples of what is called protective resemblance and have grown to match the colour of sand and rocks, of trees and reeds, where they live. The hoofs of some are perfect for hill-climbing, those of others ideal for speed over sands, or boggy marshlands, or even stretches of ice and snow. Cattle, sheep, goats, antelopes and deer all have hoofs and may be horned. They are all called ruminants, because they have a special kind of stomach. They swallow their food in haste and then chew it again when they are resting. This is known as chewing the cud. Antelopes have horns made of almost solid bone and some of them, as in the case of Gemsboks, are long, sharp-pointed swords which can fight off an attacking lion. From birth to death, the graceful antelopes lead hunted lives, but life is not terrible to these splendid creatures. They are born with their sense of danger highly developed. They know that there may be lions all around them, but have faith in their own protection of keen sight, scent, hearing and speed.

The Springbok is the national emblem of South Africa. It gets its name from its habit of leaping suddenly into the air.

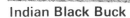

Indian Black Buck

The Gemsbok has long, sharp horns to fight off lions.

African Wildebeeste, or Gnu

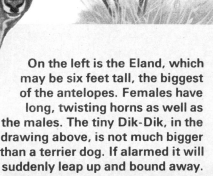

On the left is the Eland, which may be six feet tall, the biggest of the antelopes. Females have long, twisting horns as well as the males. The tiny Dik-Dik, in the drawing above, is not much bigger than a terrier dog. If alarmed it will suddenly leap up and bound away.

8

There are several different members of the Giraffe family. They vary in colour, markings, shape and the number of short horns which they have on their heads.
While its height is necessary to reach the tops of the tall trees which it feeds on, it does make going for a drink a complicated business. Even its long neck does not help very much. In order to reach the water it has to place its fore legs wide apart, then bend at the knees before it can lap up the water.

The giraffe is the tallest animal in the World and stands 18 to 19 feet high. It can be over nineteen feet tall and its neck alone is about seven feet long, longer than a tall man. Although it has such a long neck, it has only the same number of neck bones as other animals, but each bone is much longer.

The horns of the Giraffe are short and stubby. The core is made of bone which is covered with hard skin and has tufts of bristly hair at the tip.

The giraffe makes its home in the open scrub and grassland, where there are trees and shrubs for it to feed off. They eat the leaves and their long necks help them to reach the juicy leaves at the top of the trees. Their long tongues can reach up another eighteen inches, to grasp and pull off the leaves. A giraffe can go for some days without water, as long as it gets the moisture from the juicy leaves.

Under the trees, its mottled coat, long limbs and narrow body, blend best with the moving patches of shadow and the spindly trunks and branches. When they stand quite still, giraffes are often mistaken for old, gnarled forest trees, their bodies being hidden by the bushes and their long legs looking like tree stumps. The giraffe has very good eyesight and because of its height, it

Giraffes can run at great speed—thirty miles an hour or more, so they are hard to catch.

THE LONGEST LEGS IN THE WORLD!

A giraffe does not like to get wet. It will neither swim nor wade through a river in its path and shelters under the trees from the rain.

can see for a long distance. At the first sign of danger, the whole herd of giraffes gallops away. They like to live in herds of up to fifty animals.

Apart from man, the giraffe's only enemy is the lion. However, even a lion will rarely attack a giraffe on its own, for the giraffe defends itself fiercely. One blow from its powerful hoof can kill the lion and the only giraffe the lion can hope to kill on its own, is a young one which has strayed from the herd. When two giraffes fight, they use their heads as clubs, banging their long necks against each other until the victorious giraffe has knocked its opponent silly.

The only living relation of the giraffe is the Okapi, which lives in the forests of Central Africa. The trees and shrubs grow at a much lower level in the forests so the Okapi does not need such long legs and neck as the giraffe does to reach its food. However, like the giraffe, it has a long tongue, so long that it can lick its own ears.

Okapi are very timid creatures, keeping to the densest parts of the jungle. They conceal themselves by remaining quite still in the vegetation, their colour mingling so that it is impossible to see them. So complete is this camouflage that they were not discovered until 1901. Unlike the giraffe which has no voice at all, they make a noise rather like that of a cow.

THE CAT FAMILY

There are big cats and little cats, from lions and tigers down to the cats we keep in our homes as pets. They all have something in common. For beauty, grace, strength, speed and fierceness there is no other living animal to better them. They are flesh-eaters and spend their lives in the skilful hunting and killing of other animals, mainly those which feed on grass and vegetation.

Head of the family and usually known as the king of beasts is the African lion, more about which is contained on page 5 of this book. The American lion, known as the Puma, or Cougar, is shown in the large picture on the opposite page. With it are other creatures of the same region—Bison, Bald Eagle, Prong-horn, Marmot, Coyote and Jack Rabbit. Like most of the large cats, the puma seeks its prey mainly by night and the North American puma will eat almost anything, from deer down to rats, mice, fish and even snails and porcupines. It will never attack human beings and it is a fact that in places where pumas abound it is perfectly safe for a child to wander alone and even sleep on the ground. The general colour of the puma's fur is tawny, with white parts on the under body and around the mouth. The back of the ears is usually black. The colour of young puma cubs is very different, the fur on the body being marked with large blackish spots, while the tail is ringed with the same colour. These spots and rings remain distinct until the cub is about six months old and then disappear.

Tigers are found in India and most of the countries of South-East Asia. They live in forests and grassy plains, where there are plenty of other animals to hunt for food. Unlike pumas, a tiger will attack human beings when it becomes old and too slow-moving to catch the swift-footed animals which are its usual food. A man-eating tiger becomes a great terror and is very difficult to kill, for it is clever and cunning. The Lynx is easy to tell from other members of the cat family. It has long, thick legs and broad feet, its ears have a long plume, tipped with black and it has a black end to its stumpy tail. Its big yellow eyes catch the slightest movement of other animals at night and its pointed ears listen for rustling sounds. Lynx cubs, like tiny kittens, are born blind and the mother hides them away in a lair among the rocks, where enemies will not find them. A lynx does not attack humans and young cubs which are captured soon become tame and friendly, but they are so strong and their claws so sharp, that playing with them is not very easy. The domestic cat has no problems when it comes to looking after kittens. Most of them live in a good home, where comfort and food are provided. Cats were first kept, many hundreds of years ago, to catch rats and mice which lived in stores of grain and other supplies of our food.

A house cat carries one of its kittens in its mouth. Though there is no real need, its kittens will be taught how to hunt birds and small animals.

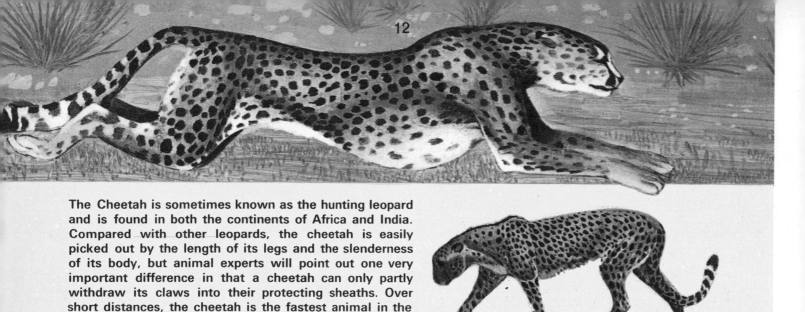

The Cheetah is sometimes known as the hunting leopard and is found in both the continents of Africa and India. Compared with other leopards, the cheetah is easily picked out by the length of its legs and the slenderness of its body, but animal experts will point out one very important difference in that a cheetah can only partly withdraw its claws into their protecting sheaths. Over short distances, the cheetah is the fastest animal in the World. Able to move at 60 miles an hour, a cheetah can catch birds on the ground before they can fly away.

Continued from page 11.

If you see a tiger in the zoo, you may think that its striped and brightly-coloured coat of fur is easily seen, but in jungles and grasslands, where it lives, the tiger is difficult to detect at a glance. Sunlight, shining through leaves and branches, makes patches of bright light and dark shadow. The tiger's golden-coloured coat, with its dark stripes, blends well into these patches of sunlight and shadow. This camouflage, as it is called, is very useful to the tiger when it is out hunting. The tiger is very strong and if it kills a deer or a cow, it will often drag the dead animal several hundred yards to the shelter of some bushes, where it can eat its meal in peace. Tigers do not like great heat and when it is very hot, they find a resting place by a river or swampy ground. The tiger watches warily, on the alert for danger, as it drinks at a river. It is a very good swimmer

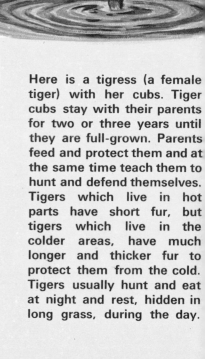

Here is a tigress (a female tiger) with her cubs. Tiger cubs stay with their parents for two or three years until they are full-grown. Parents feed and protect them and at the same time teach them to hunt and defend themselves. Tigers which live in hot parts have short fur, but tigers which live in the colder areas, have much longer and thicker fur to protect them from the cold. Tigers usually hunt and eat at night and rest, hidden in long grass, during the day.

and can cross fast-flowing rivers easily. It will plunge into a river to escape from its enemies, or other dangers, such as bush-fires. It uses teeth and claws to defend itself, but unlike some of the other cats, is not a very good climber.

A member of the cat family which is very much at home in trees is the Leopard. It can run up a straight-stemmed and smooth-barked trunk with the agility of a monkey. In point of size it comes third in the cat family—after tigers and lions. Like the lynx, the leopard is found in more parts of the World than the other wild cats, being seen in the whole of Asia apart from Northern Siberia, most of the Indian sub-continent, the islands of the Malay region, the Arabian countries and a great part of Africa. The spotted coat of the leopard is its most marked feature. These spots vary in size and number. The smaller ones are a solid dark colour, the larger ones usually being in the form of an incomplete circle. When first looking at a picture or photograph of a "spotted" wild cat, the question is often asked . . . is it a leopard or a jaguar? This is a question that would never arise in the wild, for they are not found in the same parts of the World. The Jaguar, shown below, lounging in the warmth of the jungle, lives in South America. Compare the spots and you will see that a jaguar has larger and fewer spots and they are of a different pattern. The jaguar also has a slightly larger head. Big and powerful, the jaguar will attack and eat almost any bird or mammal that crosses its path. Its favourite prey is a little South American pig-like animal called a peccary. The jaguar is the best of all cats at tree-climbing and its most-used method of hunting is to lurk in the branches of a tree, wait until an unsuspecting animal appears on the ground below, then plunge down upon it in a smothering leap. The name jaguar comes from a South American Indian word, "jaguara", which means "carnivore that overcomes its prey in a single bound". Whether hunting from the ground or from trees, this is a very accurate description of the jaguar and makes this cat greatly feared by smaller creatures living in the same area.

The front feet of all cats are provided with five toes each, whereas the hind feet have only four toes. On the end of these toes are curved and sharp claws and, with the one exception of the hunting leopard, these claws can be drawn back into sheaths for their protection when not in use. To keep their claws sharp and clean, most cats—from the tigers to the house cat—draw them down the bark of trees.

The leopard feels quite at home, perched high in the branches of a tree, watching what goes on below. It is the third largest of the cats.

Bigger and more powerfully built than the cats we keep as pets in our homes, these Wild Cats are from the Highland areas of Scotland. They are such fierce and savage creatures that they have never been made tame by human beings.

Jaguars are the best tree-climbers of all the cat family and generally catch their prey by pouncing upon a passing animal from a tree-branch. The one shown below, however, appears content to rest on the ground in the warm South American jungle.

Birds, mountain hares, mice and other small animals are the food of the lynx. Here, one is bringing back a meal to its two cubs in a lair among rocks. The two cubs are about half-grown and they will soon be ready to join in a hunting party.

AFRICAN BLACK RHINO

WHITE RHINO

THE RHINOCEROS

There are five types of rhino altogether, two from Africa and three from Asia. Here you can see the African pair, with the black rhino at the top of the picture and the white rhino shown below. Neither is the colour that its name suggests, although the white rhino is a lighter grey. All rhinos love to take dust and mud baths and so, after a while, they tend to take on the colour of the soil where they live. Their food consists mainly of leaves and small shoots. Both the African rhinos have two horns, the front horn being longer than the other. Unlike other horned animals, the horns of the rhino are not really horns at all, but are made from very tough hair fibre, growing out of its skin.

Unfortunately, these rather magnificent horns have been the downfall of the rhino, as there is still a mistaken belief among the people of the backward countries, where the rhinos live, that the horns possess some magic quality that wards off evil. For this reason, many thousands of rhinos have been killed by poachers. As a result, the white rhino has become very rare and the number of black rhinos is becoming less and less.

INDIAN RHINOS

The Indian rhino, above, is second in size only to the white rhino of Africa. Unlike African rhinos, it has only one horn and the skin is thicker and hangs in folds. Indian rhinos like to live in swampy places, near to water. Their chief enemy is the tiger, but even tigers only attack the young calves when the mother rhino is safely out of the way.

Smallest of all rhinos is the little Sumatran rhino. It is only about four feet high and is also the only one with a hairy coat. It is found in the dense forest areas of Sumatra and Borneo. Like the others, this kind is also dying out and, as far as we know, there are only about a hundred of them left in the World.

Rarest of all rhinos is the Javan rhino, a smaller relative of the Indian. There are now less than fifty Javan rhinos in existence. Game reserves and sanctuaries for all five types are now helping the rhino to survive, in the hope that these magnificent creatures will not die out altogether.

The little Sumatran Rhino above looks quite cuddly with its long hair. Rhinos are grazing animals, eating grasses and foliage like the Java Rhino below.

THE DOG FAMILY

Although man has managed to tame many breeds of dog, there are still plenty of wild canines left roaming around in various parts of the World. These animals live in much the same conditions as their common ancestors, hunting singly or in packs, howling and yelping rather than barking and living in burrows, clefts, caves or hollow trees. Dogs, which we keep as pets,

The Fox is found in countries all over the world. Foxes are nocturnal, which means that they hunt and feed during the night and sleep by day. Their prey includes small birds, rabbits and poultry.

The Spotted Hyena comes from Africa. Some people dispute that it is a member of the dog family. A cowardly animal, the hyena does not hunt for itself, but eats the remains of another animal's kill.

The Jackals live in hot countries, such as Africa and Southern Asia. They roam at night, in search of carrion and small animals, but also eat fruit. The Asiatic breed is seldom more than 26 inches long, but the African jackal grows to over four feet. Long-furred and bushy-tailed, the Coyote comes from North America. It is seldom dangerous to anything except poultry. The tiniest of all the foxes is the little Fennec Fox of North Africa. Only fifteen inches long, it has enormous ears. Fennec foxes are clever and easily tamed, so they make delightful pets.

COYOTE

JACKALS

FENNEC FOXES

are often very clever. Some wild members of the dog family are very clever also. With the exception of the hyena, they are all hunters and they sometimes show great cunning, both when hunting other animals for food and in escaping their own enemies. One of the most beautifully coloured of the wild dogs, some say of the entire animal kingdom, is the fox. Its coat is a rich, reddish brown and white in colour, with black streaks and patches behind its ears and on its legs. These colours help to hide the fox, as they blend in well with the leaves, branches and shadows of the forests and hedgerows where it lives. On these pages, you can learn some more fascinating facts about the fox and other members of the dog family.

The Dingo is a wild dog which lives in Australia. Dingoes do not live or hunt together in packs, preferring to go alone or in pairs. They are unpopular with farmers, as they kill sheep.

The Cape Hunting Dog, sometimes called the hyena dog, lives on the African plains and hunts in packs, preying on herds of antelope. Its strange, tortoise-shell coat of yellow, black and white patches, is irregular in pattern, so that no two cape hunting dogs look the same. Rounded, upstanding ears distinguish it from the other canines. The Wolf is the largest wild canine. Once abundant in Britain, it now exists only in northern areas of the World. It hunts in pairs, preying chiefly on flocks and using its powerful teeth to rend victims. The European wolf, which is a forest dweller, is brownish-grey in colour, while the American species is greyer.

CAPE HUNTING DOGS

WOLVES

THE HIPPOPOTAMUS

Swimming on the surface or walking on the river's bed, hippos are always at home in water.

The name hippopotamus comes from two Greek words and means river horse, but the hippo is really a relative of the pig, from which we get our bacon. A very long time ago, hippos lived in England and Europe, for we have found their remains, but now they live only in Central Africa. They are the biggest land animals, except for elephants and weigh about four or five tons. Hippos like water and they can swim much faster than they can walk. A hippo is like a large submarine, it can close up its ears and nostrils, so that they are watertight and then walk about on the bottom of the river, searching for food. It can stay on the bottom for five or ten minutes before it has to come up to breathe. Here is a hippopotamus with its huge mouth wide open. It needs a big mouth to take in plenty of food, for it can eat up to 400 pounds of food in one day. It only eats plants and the big tusks you can see in its bottom jaw are used for digging up water plants which it brings to the surface to eat. The hippo used to be hunted for its valuable tusks, which give us ivory and at one time the tusks were used for making false teeth.

Hippopotamus babies can walk and swim soon after they are born. The mother takes great care of her baby. She takes it to the water and teaches it to find food and gives it a ride on her back when it is tired, as you can see in the top-left picture. The baby enjoys this, for it cannot stay

underwater as long as its mother and has to keep bobbing up to the surface for air. A hippo is quite happy to spend most of the day floating lazily in the water, with only its eyes and nostrils showing. It does not like to stay out in the hot sun, for the heat fries its skin and makes it crack. On the right is a basking hippopotamus which has been joined by several birds called egrets. These birds pick insects off the hippo's hide which might harm or annoy it. The birds get a free meal and the hippo gets rid of the insects. The birds often stay near the herd of hippos and move around with them. They are useful, for the hippo's sight is poor and the alarm call of the bird warns the hippo when danger is near.

At night hippos come ashore to feed on grasses and shrubs. Sometimes they find cultivated fields and then they make a meal of sugar cane, rice, maize or corn. They eat a large part of the crop and destroy much more with their big feet as they wander around a field, but they can also be very useful. It takes a huge supply of plants to feed a hippo and by eating the plants which grow on the bottom of the rivers and lakes, they keep the rivers clear and prevent them from being choked with mud and weeds. Hippos are usually quite placid, but sometimes they do become dangerous and rush upon a passing boat, trampling it under water or chewing it up with their big teeth.

Hippopotamus babies can walk and swim soon after they are born. The mother takes great care of her baby, and teaches it how to find food in the water.

One of the strangest sights in Nature is to see the unusual partnerships that are to be found among animals. Above, egrets feed off the insects buried in the hippo's hide which otherwise might harm it. Thus, the birds are provided with a meal, while the hippo's unwelcome visitors are removed!

With their large appetite for plants, hippos, below, help to stop rivers and lakes from becoming choked by weeds.

CAMELS—THE SHIPS

The camel is often called the "ship of the desert", for in the hot desert areas of Africa and Asia where there are no roads and railways, the only way of carrying goods and people long distances is by camel. Camels are of two kinds. The one below is a Bactrian camel, which has two humps. The one on the right is an Arabian camel. It has only one hump and is also called a dromedary. Camels have been used by man for many hundreds of years.

Bactrian camels come from Central Asia, China and Southern Siberia. Here the weather is not always warm, but Bactrian camels can stand the cold quite well. They grow a Winter coat of long, thick hair to keep them warm.

The Bactrian camels are longer in the body than the Arabian camels opposite and, as you can see, they have shorter legs. Also, their feet are harder, for they live among rocky, hill country and they often have to climb steep slopes with their loads. They feed on the thorny, bitter-tasting plants which other animals cannot eat and drink happily from lakes of brackish, salty water. Because these animals are so hardy and can stand both heat and cold, they are very valuable to the nomads (people who spend their lives wandering from place to place) who live in Asia. Camels are bad-tempered animals and they never show any affection for their human masters.

OF THE DESERT!

Many of the Arabs who live in the hot, dry desert areas of Africa and Asia spend their lives wandering around from oasis to oasis (an oasis is a place where there are wells of water and palm trees growing). They keep herds of Arabian camels, which are the most valuable animals in this part of the World. Arabian camels have long legs and wide, soft feet like cushions, which spread out as they walk over the soft, sandy ground so that they do not sink in.

The camel will happily travel long distances, with a heavy load, across the hot, dry desert, but it will only cross even the smallest stream when it is forced to do so, for the one thing it dislikes is crossing water.

Camels can eat the toughest and thorniest desert plants and when there is plenty of food to eat, they store the extra food in the form of fat in their humps. They live on this fat when food is scarce. They also store water in the cells lining their stomachs and they can travel without water for about three days. In the desert, where there is little food and water, this is very useful. Camels are used for riding and carrying baggage and, unlike horses, they can close their eyes and ears against the desert sand in a sandstorm. The Arabs drink the camel's milk, weave its hair into cloth and rope and eat its flesh as we eat roast beef.

The first men to come to Australia, many hundreds of years ago, were the aborigines. They were hunters and brought with them their hunting dogs, some of which ran wild and became ancestors of the Wild Dingoes which live in Australia today. The picture shows an aborigine hunter and his dog, both wondering if the nearest kangaroo will bound away like the rest.

STRANGE ANIMALS OF AUSTRALIA

A Great Grey kangaroo with a baby in her pouch. Notice how kangaroos often "sit on" their thick tails.

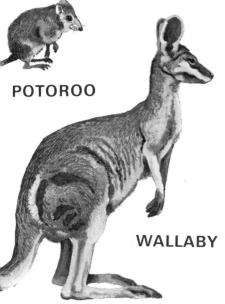

POTOROO

WALLABY

The animals of Australia are very different from those in the rest of the World. They come from an earlier age and their shapes and forms seem strange. This is because Australia became cut off by sea from other parts of the World millions of years ago and its animal life has developed more slowly than elsewhere. Australia's best-known animal is the Kangaroo, famous for the way in which it uses its long back legs to move around in great leaps. Altogether there are more than 20 different kinds of kangaroos and their smaller relative, the wallaby, living in Australia and New Guinea today. The most common is the Great Grey kangaroo. Biggest in size is the Red kangaroo. Smallest is the Potoroo. The Red kangaroo is about as tall as a man and with its powerful hind legs it is able to leap along at speeds of up to 25 miles an hour, often covering a distance of 8 yards in a single leap. Kangaroos are usually shy and timid animals, but they often stray into a farmer's fields to eat his crops of wheat or oats, for a fence 8 or 9 feet high can easily be jumped by a kangaroo. A baby is born to the female in Spring. It is about an inch long when born and lives in its mother's pouch until big enough to bound along beside her. Animals such as kangaroos, which carry their young in pouches, are called marsupials.

RED KANGAROO

The Yellow-footed wallaby, about three feet tall, lives in the more mountainous regions of Australia.

This Tree kangaroo prefers to live in trees, leaping from branch to branch, often jumping 30 feet.

Other Strange Animals of Australia

GLIDER

KOALA BEAR

WOMBAT

ECHIDNA

MARSUPIAL CAT

TASMANIAN WOLF

Kangaroos are not the only strange animals to be found in Australia. Among others is the little Koala bear. They were probably the models for our cuddly toy teddy-bears, but although we call them bears, they are not related to real bears at all. Koalas are about two feet tall. They have round faces, with bright beady eyes, flat rubbery noses and fluffy ears. They have strong claws, with which they can tightly grip the branches of the eucalyptus trees, feeding on the leaves. The baby Koala, only about three-quarters of an inch long when born, stays in its mother's pouch for about six months, until it is able to cling to her back and be carried around. These animals were given the name Koala by the aborigines. In their language the name means "stupid, or very silly fellow", but although they are gentle and slow-moving, Koalas are not at all stupid. The Glider, seen above, is a squirrel-like creature that is able to spread its legs like a parachute and glide from one branch to another among the tree-tops.

From the forests of South Australia comes the Wombat, a bear-like animal that feeds on plants and has very strong claws for digging. The spiky creature below it is an Echidna, which feeds on termites and searches for them in the ground with its pointed snout. The Marsupial cat, as its name suggests, means that it has a special pouch, like a kangaroo, in which to carry its babies.

The Tasmanian Wolf, which is now becoming very rare, comes from Tasmania, an island just off the Australian coast. The Black Tasmanian Devil looks rather fierce, doesn't it? It is also now only found in Tasmania, though once it could be seen roaming all over Australia. The Banded Ant-Eater comes from the South Australian forest and, as its name suggests, feeds on termites, or ants.

Where there is some water around, you are most likely to find what is probably the weirdest of all creatures in the World—the Duck-billed Platypus. This strange animal, with a beak like a duck, can stay under water for up to ten minutes at a time, feeding on pond life, snails and worms.

These are just some of the strange animals which live in Australia.

BANDED ANT-EATER

TASMANIAN DEVIL

DUCK-BILLED PLATYPUS

THREE BEARS

Do not be misled by the heavy, cumbersome appearance of bears, for they are remarkably agile animals. Expert swimmers and great mountaineers, they think nothing of crossing snow-capped mountain peaks and will travel long distances in search of food.

Polar Bears are the fiercest of all bears and they have been known to hunt men across the ice-floes of the Arctic seas where the bears live. Seals are their natural food, but they also eat seaweed and other growing plants in Summer. Female polar bears often find themselves a snug den in Winter and there they give birth to their cubs. If there is any danger, a mother bear will defend her cubs fiercely, even if she is wounded.

The largest of all bears is the Grizzly, above, which may be over nine feet tall when it stands on its hind legs. It lives in North America and Canada and feeds on small animals, grubs and plants. It has a very bad temper and can be very dangerous when alarmed. In the days when only Red Indians lived in North America, the highest badge of courage an Indian warrior could have was a necklace made from the claws of Grizzly bears which he had killed. Many years ago, European Brown Bears roamed the forests of Britain, but nowadays they are only found in the mountains between France and Spain, Norway and Russia. They feed on berries, roots and small animals and they can swim, climb trees and move swiftly over the ground.

THE DEER FAMILY

For many, many centuries, deer have roamed wild over most parts of the World. The earliest men, who lived in caves, hunted the deer, for they needed its meat for food, its bone antlers for weapons and its hide for clothing. There are still herds of wild deer in most parts of the World and they are among the most swift and graceful of all animals. Here and on the next three pages, you can learn about some of them. Top left, is a strange little deer called a Muntjac.

continued in next column

BARKING DEER

MUSK DEER

CHITAL

SAMBAR

CHEVROTAIN

PERE DAVID'S DEER

The deer on the left is called Pere David's Deer. A few herds of this species are kept in England, but they have never been found wild. They originally came from a herd of animals kept by the Emperor of China in his hunting park, nearly a hundred years ago. On the right is a Mule Deer, from North America. They have large, mule-like ears.

MULE DEER

A simpler name for it is the Barking Deer, because its call, when it is alarmed, sounds like the bark of a dog. The people of India and China, where it lives, rarely see it, for it is very shy and hides deep in the forest. Below it is the Musk Deer, which depends on its swiftness of foot to escape its enemies. It lives in the snowy, mountain areas and its wide feet spread out like snowshoes and carry it easily over the loose, soft snow. An enemy, like a leopard, will flounder helplessly and

Continued on next page.

REINDEER

WAPITI

The Reindeer living in the cold Northern lands, is the only deer that is tamed by man. They are kept in large herds to provide food, clothing and transport. The big, yet graceful Wapiti comes from North America.

Biggest of all the deer is the Moose, which is found both in Europe and North America. It swims around happily, searching for juicy reeds and water plants to eat. It grows into a big, powerful, rather ugly animal, always ready for a fight and it will even drive away big bears with blows from its antlers, which are six feet wide.

soon give up the chase. Both the pretty, spotted Chital and the big, sturdy Sambar deer live in the area around India. Most male deer have big spreading antlers and, if you turn back one page, you can see two Chital stags in the big picture, using their antlers to fight a battle, crashing their heads together so that their antlers meet with a powerful shock, until one of them is knocked silly. The shy little Chevrotains come from India and Ceylon, but spend most of their time hiding in the tangled forest undergrowth. Roe and Fallow Deer, seen on this page, are both found in England. The roe deer, top left, is another shy animal. It lives in woodland and moves round mostly at night. On the whole, roe deer tend to stay in family groups, in preference to living in a herd like the fallow deer. Most young deer are born with spotted coats, as in our picture on the left. This makes it harder for their enemies to spot them against the background of sunshine and shadow. A baby roe deer is called a kid. A baby fallow deer is a fawn. The third species of wild deer found in Britain is the Red Deer, found mostly in the mountains of Scotland. You can see some pictures of the red deer on the opposite page. In September, when their antlers have grown big and strong, the stags rub them against the tree branches, to remove the velvet covering. Now is the time for the stag to find itself several mates and it gathers together as many females, or does, as it can. Two stags will often fight over the ownership of a herd of does, crashing heads fiercely, until one is beaten.

Fallow Deer are found in our woodlands. In Summer, their coat is marked with large, white spots, which disappear in Winter. They are very fond of horse chestnuts, which the stags knock from the trees with their antlers.

There is no more impressive sight for the visitor to Scotland than that of a herd of red deer, roaming the highlands.

In the picture above, an old red deer stag wallows in a mountain stream. A younger stag keeps watch from the bank. You can tell that the stag on the bank is younger, for his antlers are smaller and have less branches. Each year, in the Spring, the stag's antlers drop off, but new ones soon begin to grow. They get bigger, year by year, until they reach full-size when the stag is about eight years old. The little pictures on the left show how this happens.

THE MAD MARCH HARE

Many centuries ago some animals decided that the safest place to live was in a hole in the ground where their enemies could not easily reach them. The hare does not do this, and has to rely on keen hearing and strong legs to escape from danger. The muscles of its back legs are very strong indeed, enabling it to take great leaps. When danger really threatens, the hare can achieve a speed of around forty miles an hour.

On the left you see a hare in its "form" where it crouches to rest and sleep on flattened grass. In mountainous country it sometimes lives among the rocks. Its fur, being a brownish-grey in summer, blends with the background so that it cannot easily be seen by its enemies. But in the winter when the snow is on the ground, as you can see in the picture on the right, the coat changes to white to match the snow.

Why is it called "the mad March hare"? At times hares go leaping and frisking madly about a field, but this happens in other months besides March, so the real reason for the name is not clear. On the right you can compare the hare and the rabbit. The hare is nearest. Notice how much longer its back legs are, and its ears too.

The hare lives mostly on corn, vegetables and the bark of young trees, so you can understand that it is not very popular with the farmer!

THE TIMID RABBIT

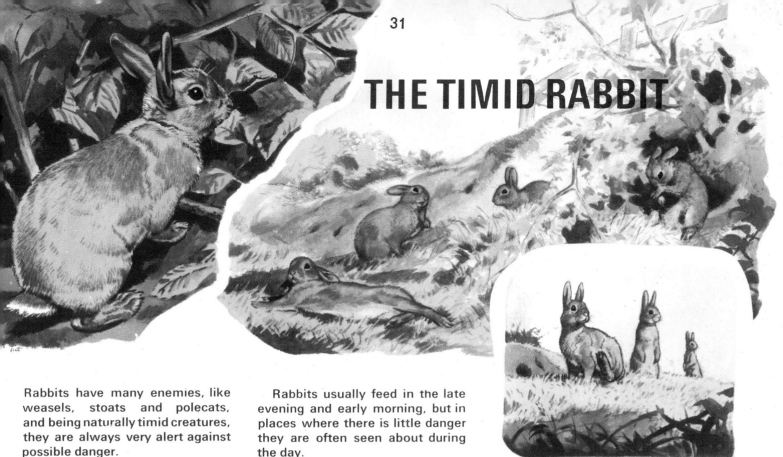

Rabbits have many enemies, like weasels, stoats and polecats, and being naturally timid creatures, they are always very alert against possible danger.

Although they live in the open country they are always near bushes, gorse and grass where they cannot easily be seen.

In the top picture on the right the leader has sensed danger and is thumping the ground with its hind leg—a signal to the others to make for their holes in the ground, called warrens.

Below that picture you can see leaders making for the warrens. Their tails, being pure white, act as a guide to the others.

Rabbits usually feed in the late evening and early morning, but in places where there is little danger they are often seen about during the day.

We do not know when the rabbit first appeared in the British Isles but it is thought to have been brought here in Roman times, and by the 12th. century existed in large numbers.

As rabbits have their young about four times a year, and have their own families when they are six months old, they multiply very quickly. It is said that one pair of rabbits could have 13 million descendants in three years!

Here you see rabbits feeding—they live on grass, corn, vegetables and the bark of trees. On the right they are in a warren—a hole burrowed in the ground. Here their babies are born, blind and naked at first, but they grow very quickly and are soon digging their own warrens to live in.

TERRORS WITH THE[

LEMMINGS

The Lemming is only one of a very large family called "Rodents". The name Rodent comes from a Latin word *rodo*, which means "I gnaw". All the 2000 species in this group tear constantly with their teeth, and it is this that distinguishes them from all other animals.

The Lemming is a strange and fascinating creature. Small, fat, cheeky-looking, he makes his home in the heights of the Norwegian mountains. He looks rather like a Golden Hamster, but more bad tempered! His angry squeaks and grunts are meant to scare off his enemies, and the little Lemming has many of these. As he is only five or six inches long, he really has little defence against more powerful foes. At least his thick fur protects him from the ice and snow. Choosing ground which is well drained and fairly dry, the Lemmings dig a shallow burrow and during daylight hours they sit outside, ready to vanish if danger should threaten. Sometimes, their numbers increase so fast that there is not sufficient food for them all. When this happens, they move down to the lower slopes, into the cornfields and meadows below. On their way, they are attacked by foxes, owls and eagles, but press ever onward, over lake and river, in their search for food.

The eyes of a Lemming can see but a little way ahead, so when it finally reaches the sea or a wide lake, it does not see the vast stretch of water in front and plunges in at once. It believes it has only a small river to cross. Many thousands follow and swim on until they are exhausted and drown. A sad end for the little Lemming.

COYPU

The Coypu, sometimes called the Beaver Rat, lives in South America and the West Indies. He is quite a big chap, measuring about two feet long, and with the powerful gnawing teeth of the rodent family. The Coypu is bred for its fur, and was introduced into England for this purpose in the 1930's. It became destructive and is now regarded as vermin.

CHIPMUNK

This little fellow is also known by another name—the ground squirrel. At first glance, his head is somewhat like that of a rat or mouse, but the Chipmunk is a quite different species. A second glance at his *tail* shows that! Furthermore, you will not find a Chipmunk in Britain, unless he is in a zoo. His natural home is in the cold wastes of Siberia and also on the North American continent.

...EETH !

JERBOA

With his long legs and tail, the Jerboa reminds one of a tiny kangaroo. But he does not live in Australia. His home is the African desert.

Only about eight inches long, the Jerboa constructs a small burrow in the sand where it sleeps all day. It only ventures out at night in search of food.

GERBIL

Here is another chap who is a terror with his teeth. The Gerbil can chop his way through his food in much the same way that a man can shave off wood with a chisel. In fact, the front teeth are shaped like curved chisels—and are quite as sharp. As fast as the tops are worn by constant gnawing, they continue to grow upwards from the roots. The Gerbil is a native to Asia and Africa, and can leap several feet.

PORCUPINE

Here is the hedgehog's big brother, the Porcupine. This very prickly fellow walks backwards to protect himself, and it is easy to see why! Those sharp spines are quite enough to make any enemy pause and think twice. His teeth are just as sharp, but he only employs them to chew his food. Perhaps you wonder what 'Porcupine' means? It comes from the French "porc", which means "pig".

SPRINGHAAS

South and East Africa is the home of the Springhaas. He too is always concerned to keep his teeth short and sharp. Like all rodents, most of his gnawing is not done for eating, but to stop his teeth from growing too long. Should this happen, the poor animal would be unable to eat and would die. About eleven inches high, the Springhaas usually moves on all fours—but can take twenty foot leaps when frightened.

COMMON SHREW

FIELD MOUSE

Here is a group of more well-known friends. All of us have seen the field mouse, and if we have watched very carefully on our country walks, we might have spotted the Common Shrew, the Short-Tailed Vole, the Bank Vole and the Dormouse.

Yes, all terrors with their teeth! Most of them live mainly on roots, stems and nuts. All are hunted by other creatures, but still they survive—and *gnaw gnaw, gnaw!*

SHORT-TAILED VOLE

BANK VOLE

DORMOUSE

Red and Grey SQUIRRELS

**In the parks and woods
watch for the lively squirrels**

Once there were only Red Squirrels living in Britain. Then, about a hundred years ago, Grey Squirrels were brought from America. The grey squirrels were bigger and fiercer than the red squirrels and wherever they went, they drove the red squirrels away, so that now there are more grey squirrels than red ones. Farmers call the grey squirrels a pest, because they damage trees and crops, by gnawing at them with their sharp little teeth, but children in the park think it is great fun to watch their lively antics as they leap and run high up in the branches of the trees. Their sharp little claws grip the trunk so tightly that they never fall. On the left is the squirrel's home. It is an untidy nest of twigs which we call a "drey".

Autumn is the time when squirrels make their larders. They make little holes in the ground and fill them with nuts, to dig up and eat in Winter, when food is scarce.

In Spring, the baby squirrels are born. They are warm and cosy in their nests, padded with moss and feathers, but they are soon learning how to leap from branch to branch,

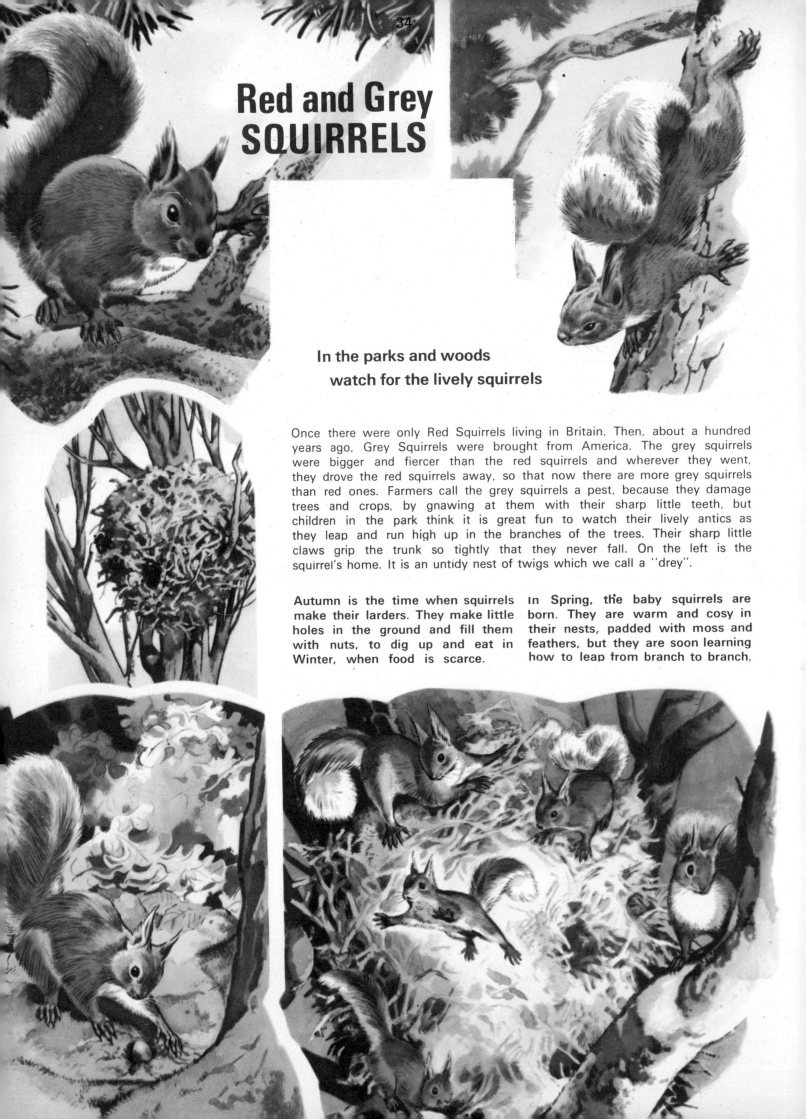

Squirrels leap so cleverly among the branches because they know how to spread out their legs and tails to give them balance. They are clever, too, at picking nuts and holding them in their front paws while they gnaw through the shell.

At a quick glance, you may think that grey and red squirrels look alike, but these pictures show you some differences. The red squirrel has tufts of hair on its ears and a smaller head, while the grey squirrel's tail is longer and thicker. Their big tails help them to keep their balance. Grey squirrels like to live in beech trees, but red squirrels like to live in pines.

The grey squirrels in the parks often become very tame. They will run down the trees to take nuts and food from people they are used to.

OTTERS and BEAVERS

The otter and the beaver are very much creatures of the water.

Otters are expert swimmers. Their short powerful legs and webbed feet help them to achieve a tremendous speed, on the surface or under it.

Usually they swim with their bodies under water and their noses above the surface. Then they spot a fish, and dive, being able to close their ears so that the water does not enter.

Nature has also given the otter fine protection against the cold. It has an outer coat which is waterproof and an inner one of thick fur.

Eels, salmon, trout and pike form their main food—but they sometimes vary the menu with a duck which falls an easy victim—they swim quietly under it and pull it down by its legs.

In the illustration on the left you see a mother otter with two of her young going down to the water. If you think the young ones look a little frightened you are right, for they are not born swimmers and have to be persuaded to go into the water to learn.

Beavers have to live where there is flowing water. Their lodge has an underwater entrance to make it safe for the young. A barrier of logs stops it from being swept away.

Beavers, too, are strong swimmers, and close their nostrils when they dive.

The beaver lives on the bark of trees and roots of plants, and mostly moves by night.

It is a wonderful engineer. In the picture above you see many beavers building their home; first damming the water with fallen tree trunks, and in the picture below you see one gnawing through the trunk with expert precision so that it falls in the right place. The bark is ripped off for food.

The lodge is made of branches and twigs covered with mud to make it warm and watertight.

The chamber itself is above water but the entrance tunnels are under the surface. This protects the baby beavers from enemies and of course the entrance can still be used even when the stream is frozen over.

THE TUNNEL BUILDERS

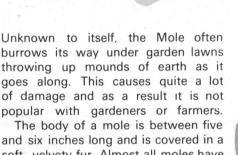

The Mole spends most of its life under the ground, searching for worms, grubs and insects that it feeds on. It cannot live for more than twelve hours without food so it is always busy, making tunnels as it burrows for food.

Unknown to itself, the Mole often burrows its way under garden lawns throwing up mounds of earth as it goes along. This causes quite a lot of damage and as a result it is not popular with gardeners or farmers.

The body of a mole is between five and six inches long and is covered in a soft, velvety fur. Almost all moles have black coats, although some have been found with cream or brown coats. Although the mole has eyes and ears, they are small and are usually covered by its furry coat. This stops loose dirt from getting into them. The mole's sharp little nose is useful for digging up grubs and worms from the roots of plants.

The nest of the mole, which is between two and six inches below the ground, is under a large mound of earth and is lined with leaves and grass. Inside this mound are many tunnels and holes leading off in all directions. The mole has made these while it has been looking for food. Some of the tunnels are quite short and do not have any openings. These are used to confuse any enemy which might attack the mole, which also has its own special escape route.

The front feet and claws are very powerful and the mole can dig very quickly.

Baby moles are usually born in early April and there are between four and six little ones in their nest of leaves.

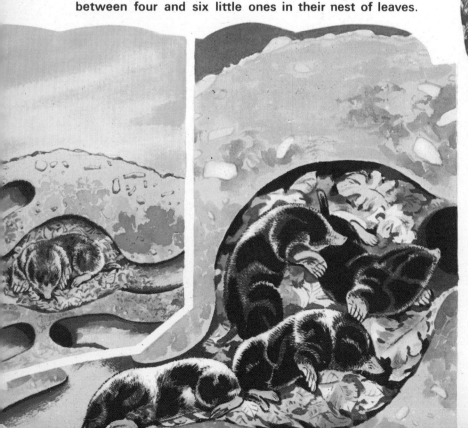

The mole makes a hole in its tunnel and pushes the waste earth up to the surface, forming the mounds. We can see its path by following these mounds. Only when its home is flooded, or it is chased by an enemy, does the mole come up to the surface.

PRICKLY PETS!

This friendly animal gets its name because it lives in the hedge and has a nose like a hog (which is another name for a pig). It is very useful in the garden because it eats the slugs and beetles that spoil the plants. It hunts for its food at night time.

The Hedgehog is covered by many prickly spines poking out through its tough coarse fur. It can roll itself up into a ball with its head and feet tucked in and its spines sticking out. This helps to protect it from dogs and foxes if they attack it. When full-grown, it measures about 10" long.

Hedgehogs eat insects, worms, snails, slugs, roots, and sometimes rats and mice and other small animals. They also eat snakes, which they kill by biting on the neck, and if the snake threatens to bite back the hedgehog simply curls up into a prickly ball. They are not popular with game-keepers because they are fond of birds' eggs.

Hedgehogs come out in the late evening to find their food, but they are sometimes seen during the day. This is probably because they have to spend much more time looking for food for their young which are born in July and August. When they are first born, hedgehogs are almost naked and completely blind, so they have to be protected by their parents for some time. They are born in a nest of moss and leaves which is very carefully made and has a roof to protect them from the rain.

When the little ones are old enough to take their first look at the world, their mother leads the way.

Hedgehogs can swim. This one is searching for frogs which it finds near the pond.

Even a high fence does not keep the hedgehog out. Using his four small paws he climbs up and over into the garden, where there is a bowl of bread and milk for him, which he loves.

When Winter comes, some animals, like the hare, have a hard time finding food. The hedgehog, however, simply curls up in his nest and sleeps until the warm weather comes again.

AS CLEAN AS A PIG!

DOMESTIC PIG

RED RIVER HOG

WART HOG

WILD BOAR

There is nothing dirty about

a pig. When it wallows in

the mud, it is only taking a bath.

BARBIRUSA

COLLARED PECCARY

The Red River Hog lives along the river banks in the damp forests of West Africa. The pigs will work together as a team to move huge, fallen trees. Then they all eat the rats, giant snails, poisonous snakes and pests they find underneath. The ugly Wart Hog gets its name from the warts on its face. Like all pigs, it loves to roll in mud. This keeps it cool and the dried mud protects it from the stings of flies. Wild Boars are fierce, dangerous animals and will attack savagely with their tusks. A few boars still live in the forests of Europe. The Barbirusas live in the Malayan swamps. They are good swimmers, and like to eat water plants. Unlike most pigs, they do not grow thick hair. Peccaries roam the forests of America. They eat roots, nuts, and sometimes snakes. Like other pigs, snake bites do not seem to harm them. Although they are small, they can be very dangerous if they all attack together in a herd. The Giant Forest Hog is an enormous pig which lives deep in the thick tropical forests of Africa and so it is rarely seen. It uses its long snout to poke among the undergrowth to find fruit and nuts to eat.

The domestic pig we know, is descended from the wild boar and was one of the first animals to be domesticated by man. Pigs were used as scavengers before it was discovered that their flesh was good to eat.

Charles Lamb, the famous English essayist, tells a story about the discovery of roast pork. The house of a Chinese who kept a pig as a scavenger caught fire and the pig was burned to death. Someone picked up a piece of burnt pig, tasted it, and found that it was good. Thereafter house after house was set on fire to roast pigs—until it was realized that pigs could be roasted without burning houses!

Pigs are among the most valuable of domestic animals, for every part of them has some use. The meat is a good food; the fat, called lard, is used for cooking; the hair or bristles make the best brushes and the skin provides a strong, hard-wearing leather for saddles, suitcases, gloves and shoes.

Among British breeds of domestic pigs are the Large, Middle and Small Yorkshire, the Lincolnshire Curly Coated, Large Black and Tamworth.

GIANT FOREST HOG

INDIA

HIMALAYAS

INDIAN OCEAN

ANIMALS OF THE HIMALAYAS

In the Himalayan range of mountains, from the warmth of the jungle foothills to the cold of high, snow peaks, many different kinds of animals live; and it is possible that there are still some to be discovered, such as the Yeti, or Abominable Snowman, which some people claim to have seen. Certainly, mysterious big footprints have been seen in the snow, which have no explanation and appear to have been made by a large, strange animal. In the main picture on the opposite page, a Snow Leopard is shown on the prowl. It is similar to the ordinary leopard, but much paler in colour, with long, plumelike tur. It is stalking one of the animals in the herd of Takin. These odd-looking creatures are related to the goat and antelope family. So far, they appear not to have seen the leopard, being far more worried by the sight of the Himalayan bear, ambling up the hillside towards them. Safe on a distant crag is a herd of Yahr goats and in the bushes in the foreground, a Red Panda, a good if slow climber, sits quietly until the danger is past.

In the cold mountain regions, one animal is so useful that Tibetans probably would not be able to survive without it. This animal is the Yak, a big, strong creature with humped shoulders and curved horns. Yaks live only in the coldest and wildest part of the country, for in spite of their heavy build they can climb the rough mountain slopes with ease. Their thick hairy coats hang nearly to their ankles and keep them warm in the coldest Winter. In fact, yaks love the icy weather and hate the heat. In places where no other form of transport is available to take people and their goods from place to place, the Tibetans have used yaks as beasts of burden for many centuries. They also use yaks in other ways, keeping large herds of them, as other countries keep herds of cows. From the yaks' milk they make butter. Yaks provide meat, their long hair is woven into cloth and their hides are used for leather. They carry riders and heavy loads through the mountains and can swim across fast-flowing rivers of icy water, surviving in barren areas where other animals would almost certainly die.

Some Tibetans have a method of passing messages to each other, by tying special knots in the long hair which hangs from the yak's belly. Other Tibetans see the knots and know what they stand for—rather in the same way that ships at sea can pass messages by using different flags.

Wild yaks roam in small herds. Their food is the tough wiry grass of the barren mountains where they live. They wander around all the time, searching for new pastures, for food is scarce.

Without yaks, travel in some parts of Tibet would not be possible. They can carry heavy loads.

DIFFERENT KINDS OF CATTLE

The gentle Watussi cattle (above) are bred by the tribesmen of Uganda, and have the largest horns of all domestic cattle. The tribesmen count their wealth by how many Watussi cattle they have. Jersey cattle (above right) first came from Jersey, one of the larger Channel Islands. Small and beautifully marked in fawn or cream with darker patches, this cow gives very rich milk. The small black cow is a Dexter, an Irish breed.

Bison are big and strong and covered with thick, shaggy hair to keep them warm in very severe Winters. In Spring they shed their thick coats and their skin is left almost bare during the hot Summer months.

Once, millions of bison roamed wild in vast herds over the plains of North America and they provided the Indians with meat to eat and warm skins for clothing. Most of them were hunted and killed and the few which are left are now protected by law.

A OXENHAM

Cattle bred to become beef have heavy, well-rounded bodies, but the milk or milch cow is lean and angular.

An average dairy cow yields six to seven quarts of milk for three hundred days in the year. Really first class animals yield nearly twelve times their own weight in milk every year.

At one time a man's wealth was judged by the number of cows he owned. In some parts of the world, particularly amongst certain African tribes, cows are still used as money.

We cannot imagine a world without cows to provide us with milk, butter and cheese. Yet man had been using cattle to haul his loads for centuries before he thought of specially breeding them for dairy products and to produce better meat.

With the advance of civilization, cattle became more important as the chief source of milk and meat for human beings. By careful selection, feeding and breeding, farmers were able to produce cattle particularly suitable for beef or milk.

Hereford cattle are reared for beef. This is an English breed but many of them have been exported to start large herds in North America and Australia.

These big, sturdy cattle were bred in Spain and taken to South America by the Spaniards several hundred years ago. They became known as the Longhorned cattle of the huge Mexican cattle ranges.

Cattle are good swimmers and water buffalo especially love to wallow in water. As water buffaloes are very strong and can stand great heat, they are used in India to do heavy work, like pulling the plough. In spite of their fierce looks, they are easily controlled by their owners.

GIANT PANDA

High in the mountains of Tibet and Western China lives the rare and rather strange-looking Giant Panda. For many hundreds of years the Chinese knew that it existed, but it was not untill 1869 that a French missionary discovered it and the panda became known all over the world. By nature, it is a very shy animal and spends most of its time hiding in trees or in the thick jungles of rhododendrons and bamboo that grow on the mountain sides. It feeds almost entirely on bamboo shoots and its jaws and teeth are well suited to crushing the stems on which the shoots grow. On each of its forepaws the panda has a thick pad of flesh which it uses as a second "thumb" to hold thinner pieces of bamboo stems while it eats the shoots. You can see a giant panda enjoying some bamboo shoots in the picture below. Since it is so rare and hard to catch, there are few pandas in captivity, but zoos in London and Moscow each owned one, while a zoo in Peking, the capital of China, is thought to have as many as ten. In 1963 and again in March, 1965, baby pandas were born at this Peking zoo, making them the first ever to be born in captivity. The "thumb" and several other features of the panda show that it is not a member of the bear family that it so closely resembles. Instead, the Giant Panda's closest relation is the Lesser Himalayan Panda, which belongs to the raccoon family.

BUSH-BABY and POTTO

There are several kinds of Bush-Baby, but they are all lively, gentle little creatures living in the African forest. They are nocturnal creatures, spending the long, hot days sleeping in their nests of leaves, high in the tree-tops. Bush-Babies have large ears, pricked up when they are alert, to catch the slightest sound and big eyes, so that they can see well in the dark. Sometimes, at night in the jungle, there is a sound like a baby crying. It comes, not from a human baby, but from the Bush-Babies making their way through the trees. They eat insects, fruit, birds and their eggs. Bush-Babies belong to the galago family as does the Potto, right. This animal also comes from Africa and is nocturnal. It is very agile, being just as happy walking upside-down under a branch as on top of it. A Potto has sharp teeth with which it gnaws through the bark of trees. It then uses its long slender middle finger to drag out insects and grubs. It also eats fruit, leaves and birds' eggs.

WILD SHEEP AND GOATS

This is the Argali, largest of the wild sheep. These magnificent creatures live high in the mountains of Central Asia. Notice the male's thick, curved horns.

Dall's Sheep are the only wild sheep that are all white. They are found in the mountain areas of Alaska and the Yukon, and their colouring provides natural camouflage, blending in with the snow-topped boulders.

Barbary Sheep come from the mountains of Africa and are easy to pick out by the mass of long hair around the throat and fore limbs. Below, you can see two males, fighting fiercely for leadership of the herd.

The Mouflon is not covered with wool, but is short-haired with a soft undercoat of wool. Once very common, it is now dying out and found only on the island of Corsica.

If you have been to the countryside, you have probably seen sheep and goats being kept on farms, but there are wild kinds of sheep and goats which you may not know about. Although the domestic breeds of the two animals are quite different, it is not so easy to tell one from the other in the wild. A general rule, although there are exceptions, is that the horns of goats grow up and sweep backwards, as opposed to the side curling of sheep. You can learn more about some of them on these pages.

The wild goat of Persia is thought to be the chief stock from which the various breeds of domestic goat came. It is noted for its brilliant sense of timing and balance, as it leaps around the craggy peaks of its native land.

The Ibex Goat, above, is another splendid creature. The males have huge, sabre-like ringed horns, often over three feet long. These horns are very hard and if two males fight, they use them like battering-rams.

The Markhor comes from the Himalayan region. As with most of the other goats and sheep, it is the male that has the big horns and in the Markhor these are spirally twisted. If straight, they would be over five feet long.

From the same area as the Markhor comes the Tahr. Unlike other goats, the Tahr has no beard and its horns are a lot smaller than in most other kinds. These goats are noted for their sure-footedness and can often be seen making death-defying leaps across the mountainous peaks in which they live.

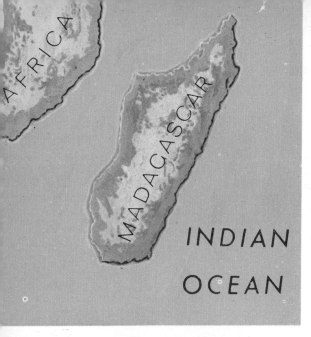

LEMURS

Lemurs are relatives of the monkey and are found only on the island of Madagascar, off the East coast of Africa. Here, cut off from almost all natural enemies, the lemurs have settled down to live quite happily. Altogether, there are ten different kinds. The smallest is only slightly larger than a mouse and the largest is as bulky as a dog. Some resemble the little bush-babies of Africa, others are more monkey-like.

The Aye-Aye, above, is the most unusual of all lemurs. This cat-like creature has very strange hands and feet. Notice how the large toe of its foot has a nail, while the other toes have claws. All the fingers of its hand are clawed, but the middle two are twice the length of the others and the third finger is very thin. This strange animal lives in Madagascar's dense forests.

The Short-tailed Indri, shown here, is very well named, because it has a small tail. Although quite slender, it is very large, sometimes over two feet in length. The face is almost dog-like and this creature is known by the natives as the "Dog of the Forest". Its most unusual features are its long-fringed ears. Vegetarians, the Indri lemurs wander about the tree-tops in groups, making a great noise with their loud, trumpet-like voices.

This is the Sifaka, the lemur that looks most like a monkey. It has often been seen resting in trees with the palms of its hands held out towards the sun. This has given rise to the strange legend of the natives that the sifaka is a sun-worshipper. Sifakas have coats in many different colours, including pure white and jet black.

Best known of all lemurs is the Ring-tailed Lemur. It is also the only one that does not live in trees, preferring to scramble around on the ground, usually among rocks. It is, of course, very easy to pick out, because of its long, bushy tail, ringed with black and white. In captivity, the ring-tailed lemur makes a very good pet. It has a strange liking for water taps and will sit for hours with its tummy under a dripping tap. Some of the natives of this island, like the three seen on the left, hunt the lemurs and are a danger to them. There is a greater danger, however, that the lemurs may die out and disappear, because more and more land in Madagascar is being used for farming and other purposes and the forest homes of the lemurs are slowly being destroyed, leaving them nowhere to live.

LAND

OF THE

TIGER

As the sun sets and the night draws near in India the animals, living in the forests and on the plains, come down to the river bank to drink. A Crocodile lies in the water watching Langur monkeys playing in the tree branches overhead and a Porcupine looks for food under a thicket. In the middle distance a shaggy, black-haired Sloth Bear lumbers out of a bamboo grove, on its way to investigate a nest of small, ant-like termites, one of its favourite foods. After breaking open the nest it will blow away the loose earth and dust and then, with great puffings and belching sounds which can be heard nearly two hundreds yards away, it will suck and lick up the unfortunate insects. Bees, leaves, flowers and fruits are other foods the sloth bear enjoys. It is an excellent climber like many of the bear family. On the ground it is not very quick on its legs and, if alarmed, will break into a clumsy gallop, usually ending when it rolls head over heels after tripping itself up. Like most other members of the bear family the sloth bear has very poor hearing and eyesight and is constantly peering about in a short-sighted manner. However, it makes up for these deficiencies with its marvellous sense of smell, enabling it to detect hidden stores of honey, or ants' nests that are many feet below the ground.

Suddenly, the scene is disturbed by a tiger. As it silently walks to the water's edge the monkeys hoot and scream their warning, a Giant Indian squirrel runs to the nearest tree, making a chirping sound and flicking its tail as it goes, while in the background two wild boars run off, knowing they are one of the tiger's favourite meals. The Chital deer, feeding on the open plain behind the wild boar, prick up their ears and look at the danger from a safe distance and two Jackals, who were about to drink, slink back among the bamboo canes. Only the crocodile, safe in the water, seems unconcerned by all the noise and confusion that has suddenly erupted, while the tiger itself just snarls at the monkeys because they gave the warning cries to the others.

THE TOPSY-TURVY SLOTH

Members of the sloth family are found only in the dense jungle regions of Central and South America. Unlike the sloth bear, the true Sloth spends its life slowly swinging upside down from branch to branch. Its four limbs have curved claws on the end, rather like grappling hooks and it moves by hooking these on to the branches, picking at its food of leaves, fresh shoots and paw-paw fruit as it goes. On the ground it becomes completely useless as it is unused to an upright position and can only sprawl about on its claws. However, it hardly ever needs to descend from its tree top home, for the sloth even sleeps hanging upside down with its head tucked in between its forepaws.

There are two types of Sloth. The two-toed one, shown at the top of the page, is about the size of a dog and has a greyish-brown coat tinged with green. The smaller, or three-toed sloth, right, has a coat that varies between silky grey and white. Even the coat of the sloth grows the wrong way so that the rain will run off it when the animal hangs upside down.

ANT-EATING ANIMALS

There are many kinds of ants in the world and most of them make their nests underground, digging tunnels and chambers to live in. The earth which the ants dig out is left on the surface in mounds. These are called ant-hills and are sometimes very large. The animals below all search for ants and termites for their food.

Termite Nests

Ant-Hills

Below is a pangolin or scaly ant-eater. It lives in Africa and eats ants and termites, which are small insects rather like ants and often called white ants. It has no teeth, but its tongue is long and sticky, for licking up ants. The pangolin is covered with hard, horny scales and can roll itself into a ball if in danger so that its enemies cannot get to it.

In South America, lives the giant armadillo which is about three feet long. It has very strong, curved front claws with which it can quickly dig ants and termites out of their nests to eat. It also digs a burrow to live in, often near an ant-hill. Giant armadillos also eat worms, snails and roots. They sometimes have as many as a hundred teeth.

This is an aardvark or ant-bear, as it is often called. It is a shy, harmless creature and spends the day asleep in its burrow. At night and in the early morning, it comes out to look for ants and termites to lick up with its long tongue. It digs very quickly with its strong front claws and its long snout is useful for probing into holes for food. It lives in Africa.

The tamandua or lesser ant-eater comes from the tropical forests of Central and South America. It can climb the tallest trees with the help of its long tail with which it grips the branches. At night it searches for the ants which live in the bark of trees and are its food. It uses its long front claws to rip open the bark and then scoops up the ants underneath on its long, sticky tongue.

The great ant-eater also lives in South America. It makes a lair in the long grass, where it sleeps during the day, with its big, bushy tail curled over its body. At night, it searches for ants' and termites' nests, which it tears open with its claws. When the ants rush to the surface, it puts its long snout into the hole it has made and sweeps the ants up in thousands on its long tongue. It has no teeth, for it does not need to chew its food.

Above: the spiny ant-eater comes from New Guinea and has a long beak-like snout. It has no teeth, and when it has dug out the ants and termites, it sucks them up into its snout through a tiny mouth. It has sharp spines among its thick coat of hair for protection against enemies. Right: the aardwolf or maned jackal lives in South Africa, and looks rather like a shaggy hyena. The thick mane of hair on its neck and back stands on end when it is frightened. It lives in a burrow with several other aardwolves and is really a very cowardly animal, running away quickly when disturbed. At night, it searches for dead animals to eat, or termites' nests which it digs out with its claws.

WILD HORSES!

Few roads cross the grey and marshy waste of the Camargue plain in Southern France, but among the treacherous saltmarshes and lagoons of the plain, the horse moves with sure-footed confidence. Across the shining, wet sands and through the marshy pools of the Camargue roam the herds of wild, white horses for which the district is famed. They gallop freely where no man would set foot, their flying hooves stirring up flocks of flamingoes, herons and rare Egyptian ibis.

Shaggy-maned, tough limbed and scarred by battles among their own herd, they move across the plain uttering their shrill calls, masters of this desolate region of hard winters and hot summers.

The horses of the Camargue are believed to be of Arab breed, introduced in medieval times by Saracen invaders who landed on the nearby coast to sweep into Spain. Some of the Saracens' sturdy little white mounts roamed riderless into the Camargue and bred there.

Apart from the horses, the plain is chiefly the home of herds of black bulls. The French cowboys of the Camargue, who guard these bulls, choose their mounts from among the wild horses.

In summer, mosquitoes torment men, bulls and horses alike. Vegetation is sparse—small clumps of junipers and shrubs half-drowned in the lagoons, or isolated groves of olives and vines near the few farms and ranches that are to be found on the plain.

ANIMALS OF THE SEAS

These animals live in the sea, but unlike fish they breathe air and their young are born alive.

The Walrus, on the left, is happy in the sea because it is a very good swimmer, but when on land it can only shuffle along, in an ungainly way, by using its flippers. It has long, pointed tusks which make it look fierce, but these are actually used for digging up shell-fish to eat.

Most of the Fur Seals were hunted and killed for their valuable fur, which is very soft, but now they are protected in many places by law. In Spring, they swim through hundreds of miles of gale-swept seas, to the place where they were born and here the new cubs are born.

Grey seals can be seen on rocky, uninhabited islands around the coast of Britain, where they often live together in small groups. Seals are very gentle creatures and are very affectionate to their pups, as the young seals are called. The pups have white fur when they are born, but this turns silvery grey, like that of their parents, as they grow older.

The Ringed Seals are found in the frozen bays and fjords of the Northern seas where there is plenty of ice. Their coats of short, thick fur keep them warm and keep the water out. The young ones are born on the ice-floes in March and April. Where the ice is solid, the seal makes itself a round blow-hole, through which it can climb to the surface and breathe, or dive deep down into the water, as it pleases. Ringed seals are the smallest in the seal family and measure about 5 feet from nose to tail.

Like the Grey Seal, the Common Seal is found around the coast of Britain. It prefers sheltered bays where the water is shallow and there are plenty of fish to eat. Baby ' seals do not take happily to the water and have to be taken there, made to go in and taught to swim and dive by their parents.

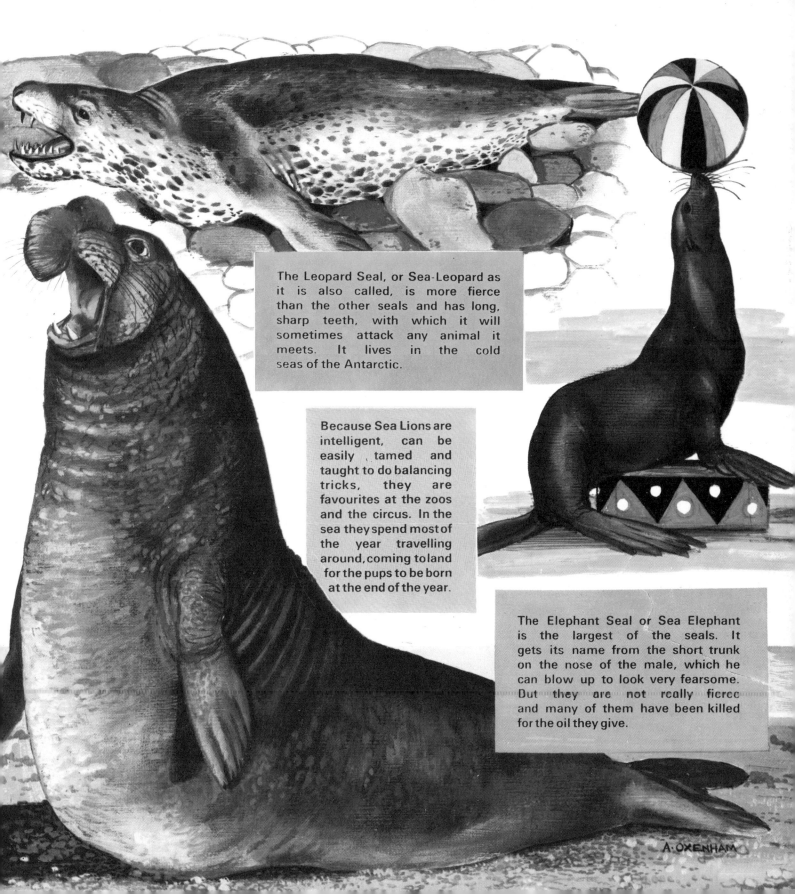

The Leopard Seal, or Sea-Leopard as it is also called, is more fierce than the other seals and has long, sharp teeth, with which it will sometimes attack any animal it meets. It lives in the cold seas of the Antarctic.

Because Sea Lions are intelligent, can be easily tamed and taught to do balancing tricks, they are favourites at the zoos and the circus. In the sea they spend most of the year travelling around, coming to land for the pups to be born at the end of the year.

The Elephant Seal or Sea Elephant is the largest of the seals. It gets its name from the short trunk on the nose of the male, which he can blow up to look very fearsome. But they are not really fierce and many of them have been killed for the oil they give.

A. OXENHAM

More animals of the seas.

Dugongs live in warm seas and although they breathe air, they can stay under water for as long as fifteen minutes. They eat seaweed and sea plants and live together in herds.

The Porpoise lives in the North Atlantic and North Pacific seas and, although it looks so much like a fish, it is really a mammal. It breathes in air through the hole on the top of its head, which is called a blow-hole. For its food it eats small fishes such as pilchards and herrings. A shoal of porpoises will often swim around a ship as it sails along and are fun to watch as they leap up out of the water.

Dolphins are slender animals about 7 feet long. They have narrow beaks and sharp teeth. They hunt together for fish to eat and a group of dolphins is called a school. They live mainly in warm seas, but are sometimes seen around the South coast of England. At one time dolphins were eaten in England for food.

The Whale breathes air ihrough a hole on the top of its head, and stays under water for about fifteen minutes before coming up to breathe again. A thick layer of fat, called blubber, underneath its skin, keeps out the cold of the water and helps it to keep warm. Whales are hunted for their blubber.

Llamas (left) and Alpacas (above) are both kept by the peasant farmers of South America.

LLAMAS AND ALPACAS

Llamas come from South America and are closely related to camels. They have the same kind of feet, with two toes ending with a hoof on each and they move in the same ungainly way as the camels. For many hundreds of years they have been used by man, not only as pack animals, but also for supplying hair, wool, hide, meat and their rather poor-quality milk. Although capable of carrying heavy loads, a llama can be very stubborn, refusing to move if it is overloaded and defending itself by spitting at its enemy. The Alpaca is another domesticated breed, descended, like the common llama, from the wild quanaco. Alpacas, usually black or all-white in colour, have very long, soft coats and of all the llama family, they are the most valuable. They are kept by the South American Indians for their wool, which is clipped once a year. The wool is made up into carpets or cloth and exported to Europe, where alpaca fetches high prices.

TAPIRS

Tapirs are found only in parts of South America and countries like Malaya and Burma. The South American tapirs, which are shown here, are dark brown. Night-time is the best time to find a tapir, for then it wanders through the jungle, looking for water plants and juicy leaves and shoots to eat. As you can see it has an odd-shaped snout, rather like a small trunk, which gives it a pig-like look. High up on the hillside, you might find a tapir's wallow, a small spring where they come to take their mud baths.

62

THE COUNTRY-SIDE AT NIGHT

PINE MARTENS

When we are asleep in the middle of the night, there are some creatures that are at their busiest. We call animals that come out at night, nocturnal animals and on this page, you can learn about some of them. In the background of the big picture on the opposite page, you see the fox, a very common sight in the countryside. It spends its day in its burrow and then comes out at dusk to feed on small birds, insects and fruit. Just clambering over the tree roots is a little hedgehog, a creature rarely ever seen during the day. It feeds on roots and garden pests, such as snails, slugs and insects. The shy roe deer is another animal that prefers the night-time for coming out into the open. In the foreground, an otter emerges from the river with its catch and the tiny water vole, or water rat as it is commonly called, goes scurrying home along the bank. One of the best-known nocturnal animals is the badger, seen in the centre of the big picture, and yet most people have never actually seen one. They are extremely shy creatures, spending all day sleeping in their sett, the name given to their home.

Even if you are out at night, they are very difficult to spot, because the black and white striped head blends so well with the patches of silvery moonlight and shadow, that it is almost invisible. Perhaps when you are in some woodlands, you may be lucky enough to find a badger's sett. It is rather like an underground mansion, with tunnels and passages which stretch for hundreds of yards. The "front door" is usually a wide hole, in a bank of earth, or close to the roots of a large tree. It will have to be in a place which is well-drained and protected from rain, though, for the badger hates damp. Together with the stoat, seen with it at the bottom of this page, the badger makes good use of its sense of smell. In the same way that rabbits and foxes use their ears, these two creatures use their noses. In fact, the stoat's sense of smell is so good that it can follow the trail of another animal without losing it, even though it might be crossed by the trails and smells of many others. Remember the next time that you are getting ready to go to sleep in your nice, warm bed, the animals you have read about on these pages will just be getting up.

After centuries of being hunted for their beautiful fur and because they are ruthless killers of poultry, the pine martens have become very scarce in Britain. This close relation of the weasel and the stoat is now only found in the Highlands of Scotland and the remoter parts of Ireland and Wales.

Most of its life is spent in trees, stalking silently from branch to branch in search of birds, squirrels and other small animals to eat. It is fond of ambushing unsuspecting creatures by hiding in a leafy bough with only its bright, beady eyes showing. With its sharp hearing it will pick up the slightest sound.

The marten's long, sharp claws give it a firm grip in the tree-tops, and the bushy tail helps the animal keep its balance when it leaps at its prey.

It generally builds its nest of straw and hay in the hollow of a tree, or takes over the nest of a large bird, adapting it so the litter of between five and seven young ones born in the spring will have a safe, cosy home.

APES and MONKEYS

Most of us think of the word "ape" as just another name for monkey, but there is a clear distinction between the two, although both belong to a group of animals called by zoologists anthropoidea.

The chief distinction between apes and monkeys is that apes do not have tails and spend most of their life on the ground. Monkeys are generally smaller than apes and commonly live in trees, where they use their tails as a kind of fifth limb when swinging from branch to branch. There are much fewer varieties of apes than there are of monkeys, but apes make up for their lack of numbers by being much more intelligent and human-like; as any one will agree who has watched a gorilla, chimpanzee or orang-utan.

The true monkey tribe numbers some hundreds of varieties. There are monkeys as tiny as squirrels and others as large as cocker spaniels. Their tails can be short and stubby, long and curly, bushy, or long and straight. There are monkeys with naked faces and others with hairy faces. Some have white cheeks, some turned-up noses. Some have tufted ears and others have ruffs round their necks, or long whiskers hanging from their cheeks.

Monkeys and apes are native to most of the warm parts of the World. They are found in India, China, Japan, Malaya, and in the tropical areas of Central and South America. At one time there were large numbers of both species in most parts of Southern Europe. Today the only native European ones are the Gibraltar apes.

The tall trees in the forests of Eastern Asia are the ideal place for these Gibbons to live. Gibbons belong to the ape family and with their long arms and legs they are able to move from branch to branch very quickly.

When captured young, Orang-Utans are playful and energetic and can soon be taught to watch and mimic people's actions. Wild adults, which are over 6 feet tall, are very fierce if angered, but the ones brought up in captivity are affectionate. They soon learn to roller-skate, ride bicycles, and even use a hammer and nails.

This big, shaggy ape, swinging happily among the branches in the tropical forest where he lives, is called an Orang-Utan. This is a Malayan word which means "Wild Man of the Woods". To see a wild orang-utan, you would have to go to the islands of Borneo and Sumatra and even here they are hard to find, for the small family parties move about the tree-tops, well hidden among the dense forests. Mid-day is feeding time and their favourite food is the juicy, evil-smelling fruit called durian, but they will also eat leaves, buds and bamboo shoots. They seldom come to the ground for their long arms and hook-like fingers make it easy for them to swing along rapidly from branch to branch in the tree-tops, while their short legs make walking a clumsy business. To drink, they dip their hands in the water and suck the drops off their fingers. At night, they build a sleeping platform of twigs.

GUINEA
BABOON

GORILLA

LANGUR

COLOBUS

The Guinea Baboon is a close relative of the mandrill baboon, right, but smaller. It lives in West Africa and in common with the mandrill is one of the few monkeys more at home on the ground. Gorillas are the biggest of apes. A full grown one is about six feet tall, but very docile! They live in the equatorial forests of the Congo. The Langur is a sacred monkey of India and is a tree-dweller living chiefly on leaves. Unlike most monkeys it can live in extreme cold. It is often seen in city bazaars helping itself to food. The Colobus, sometimes called the Guerezas, is a tree-dwelling monkey of East Africa. Its long tufts of white hair act as camouflage among the lichen growing in the damp forests.

MANDRILL BABOONS, thought by many to be the fiercest and worst tempered of all monkeys. The babies ride on their mothers' backs.

Baboons in zoos often make visitors laugh, because parts of them are so brightly coloured. There are several kinds of baboons, the two best known being the Mantled Baboon and the Mandrill. The mantled baboon, seen below is easy to pick out by the large mane which covers the neck and shoulders of the male. It is commonly found in Ethiopia and the Sudan. The mandrill, above, is one of the largest baboons and comes from West Africa. Almost tail-less, the males have long swellings on either side of their face, brilliantly coloured. Altogether, there are about a dozen different kinds, but they all come from Africa and all favour open country, rocky hillsides and ravines. They move around in large herds, or troupes, with an old male as their leader. One of their biggest enemies is the leopard, but by moving in large numbers, the baboons can usually hold their own. A group of males will sometimes even drive away the leopard. At night, the baboons take to caves or trees for added protection. Many years ago, the baboon was held by the Egyptians as sacred and it is frequently shown in old Egyptian paintings and carvings. However, there are none left in Egypt today. Baboons are mostly vegetarians, eating plants, roots, fruit and honey, but they will also eat insects and scorpions and are particularly fond of ostrich eggs. Although bold and sometimes dangerous, baboons can become quite friendly and some have made intelligent pets.

MANTLE BABOONS get their name from the mane which the male grows which looks like a short cape or mantle. Their babies cling upside down to the fur beneath the mother.

This is a Woolly monkey from the Amazon region of South America. It has thick fur and here we see it carrying a coconut with its long tail.

STRANGE MONKEYS

On the left is the Rhesus monkey. They are friendly creatures found in the North of India. Because they have much in common with human beings they have helped scientists to learn a lot about ourselves and the universe.

Below it is the Lion Tailed Macaque from Western India. Not only has it a tail like a lion but it has a mane as well.

In the column on the right, at the top, is a Golden Lion Marmoset of Brazil. Its long silky hair is a brilliant metallic gold colour.

Under it, another Brazilian monkey, the fruit-eating Squirrel monkey. It is one of the smallest monkeys and has distinctive facial markings.

At the bottom a Diana monkey from the West coast of Africa easily recognisable by the bright red streaks on each side of its back.

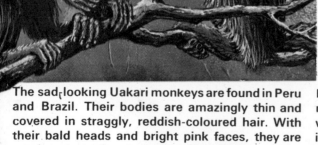

The sad-looking Uakari monkeys are found in Peru and Brazil. Their bodies are amazingly thin and covered in straggly, reddish-coloured hair. With their bald heads and bright pink faces, they are surely among the strangest of monkeys.

From Borneo, comes the Proboscis monkey. It has a very large nose, which may measure over three inches long. It loves to bask in the sun and enjoys swimming.

pider monkeys, above, get their me because they have very long ms and legs, which make them look e spiders. They use their tails like nds, to grip branches.

CLOWNS OF THE JUNGLE

himpanzees are the clowns of the ape orld. They are intelligent, inquisitive nd affectionate. In Africa they are to e found only in the jungle. Chimpanzees e in colonies, high up in the tops of e trees out of reach of their enemies hich live mainly on the ground. These es can travel for many miles without uching the ground, by walking along anches, swinging hand over hand from ugh to bough and leaping through e air from tree to tree. Their food is iefly fruit.

The mother chimpanzee looks after her baby very carefully. She builds a nest for it in the top of a tree and carries it with her while it is too young to follow on its own, the baby clinging tightly to the hair on the front of its mother.

Chimpanzees live in a very hot climate so when they are brought to zoos in Britain they have to be looked after very carefully. They are easy to teach, full of tricks and love the tea-party which so many take part in. Keepers say that

chimpanzees quickly learn perfect table manners and are extremely good at meals. The naughty tricks they play to amuse the spectators have to be taught also, otherwise they sit down like a very well behaved school outing!

INDEX

Our World is really a great ball, which revolves around the Sun and spins as it goes. To help you to look at the whole World, opposite sides are shown as separate maps, one of the New World, containing the continents of North